David Street, Jerusalem

A ~~~~ to ιne Holy Land

An artist's diary by
Margaret W. Tarrant

THE MEDICI SOCIETY LTD
LONDON 1988

At daybreak, early in March, two artists who had never before been further east than Italy, found themselves in a train speeding towards Jerusalem, and eagerly looking out for first signs of life in the Holy Land. Soon, in the dim light, came the first thrill: peasants in strange costumes were going to work in the fields and orange-groves. There were men with long robes tucked into their belts, wearing turbans or long white 'kaffiehs' (head-handkerchiefs), women with baskets on their heads, leading, perhaps, a donkey, or a camel. Here and there a primitive wooden plough was being used, drawn by donkeys, or by a mule and a cow. Certainly, this was 'the East'.

The first morning in Jerusalem will always be remembered as a vivid kaleidoscopic picture; the drive from the station, the first sight of the walls of the Holy City, new impressions, fresh scenes, strange people, costumes, smells and noises, and the excitement and novelty of it all.

I had no idea there would be so much really good costume, but there were thousands of people who looked as if they had stepped straight out of Bible stories; shepherds in striped 'abbiyehs', or in sheepskin coats, beggars who were just marvellous bunches of rags, wild-looking Arabs from the hill villages; splendid men in spotless flowing white robes, and

'basket boys' carrying incredible loads, or waiting for employment at street corners. Then there were the drink-sellers, with a strange erection of elaborate brass jugs and cups slung across their shoulders, ceaselessly rattling little metal saucers, and crying their drinks - 'Eskimo, eskimo!' meaning, I concluded, that the drinks were iced. Women in embroidered dresses squatted in odd corners, with baskets on the ground in front of them, selling oranges, vegetables, or thin chickens; others with large baskets on their heads were doing their marketing, and walking with fine swinging steps. Little children staggered along, carrying on their heads petrol-tins full of water; others dived among the people's feet, picking up dusty scraps from the road, while some, in gala costume, had evidently been brought to the city to see the sights. In the wider streets, one saw camels with great mounds of hay on their backs, donkeys with immense burdens, and cars and motor-buses, as well as humbler transport, and there were modern shops, with advertisements for 'permanent waves', or so-and-so's beauty preparations.

But always the 'suk', or native shopping-quarter, was the most interesting to English eyes. Dark little shops,

Margaret W. Tarrant

packed closely together on either side of a narrow cobbled way, the crowd jostling and shouting and merchants calling their wares. In some places the street is arched over, and is dark and mysterious, with blue smoke and strange odours issuing from the shops which provide cooked foods.

Working with a sketchbook in the streets is not an easy task. One is pushed, children and adults crowd round one, shouting, pointing, peering at one's work, obscuring any possibility of seeing the subject one is drawing. Sometimes it becomes too exasperating, and naughty children wave rags or branches in front of one so that it is impossible to continue. If one is sketching people, it is best to appear to be looking at something quite different, for either the onlookers call out to the subject to come and see, or else the subject himself comes over to ask for baksheesh.

After a busy day and the noise and turmoil of the streets, it is wonderful to go up on to a flat roof and see Jerusalem at sunset. You look across other roofs, some flat, some domed, towards the Temple Area and the Mosque of Omar, and away beyond, across the hidden Jordan Valley to the long straight line of the hills of Moab, glowing an unimaginable pink in the sunset light. Looking in the opposite direction, all the buildings stand out clear-cut and blue and romantic against the glowing sky and, from a slim and dainty Moslem minaret nearby, the muezzin chants his strange wailing call to prayer.

The country around Jerusalem is bare and stony and somewhat repellent to a stranger, but as one goes north towards Nazareth it becomes greener and more attractive, and the journey is most interesting, not only from the point of view of scenery, but from its endless historical associations. On the way, we stopped at Sychar, to see Jacob's Well where Our Lord talked to

Near the Damascus Gate, Jerusalem

3

the woman of Samaria. The well is now some distance below the level of the ground, and has a partly-built Russian Church over it with a flight of steps leading down into the small dark building.

As one's eyes become used to the swift change from the bright sunshine outside, the well becomes visible, and one notices, in the surrounding stone-work, deep smooth-worn grooves where the well ropes of centuries have run over the edge. How old are those grooves, those stones? Might they not be the actual ones which

Vegetable Market, Jerusalem

were there in the days of One who sat there and talked with the outcast woman? It is one of the best-authenticated spots in Palestine. The old monk who guards the well gives to each visitor a glass of the cold water to drink, and then he lets down a tray with some lighted candles on it, and one can watch it going down and down till the lights look like little stars in the darkness.

Much has no doubt been changed, along this way which Mary and Joseph travelled on their journey to Bethlehem, but a great deal must still be very similar – the fields, the crops, the olive trees, the groups of labouring peasants with their donkeys and camels; sunshine, flowers, the vast spaces and the long winding road so swiftly traversed in a car, but so far on foot.

The costumes of the people are noticeably different as one approaches Nazareth. The women wear brighter colours, with tight short coats and bodices, and one or two full skirts, the upper ones tucked up round their waists, and below, baggy trousers, of Turkish origin. Each district has its characteristic costume, and people familiar with the country can tell where a peasant comes from by the cut of her clothes or the way she wears her head-dress. One woman working in a field as we passed wore bright magenta trousers and an orange and yellow dress. It sounds very improbable, and had I seen it painted I should have thought it was due to the artist's vivid imagination.

We crossed the great plain of Jezreel, or Esdraelon – miles of flat country, surrounded by hills, with Mount Tabor's conical shape rising far on the northern side. This place is one of the great battle-grounds of the world, and abounds with names familiar in Bible history.

Nazareth is most beautifully situated in a hollow of the hills, 1,155 feet above sea-level; the country

Wash House in the Old City, Jerusalem

immediately surrounding the town dimly recalls the South Downs in England, and is good to look at after that around Jerusalem. There are sheets of wild flowers, making a sheen of colour among the great grey rocks beside the road – cream scabious, viper's-bugloss, with very large blue and pink flowers, a branched pink linum, large white and yellow daisies, with here and there scarlet ranunculus and many other varieties.

It is interesting to stay at the Edinburgh Mission Hospital, and to see the patients come in for treatment. Many of them travel miles on foot, on horseback, or by bus, and they seem to bring most of the other members of their families with them. These people sit about in the grounds, or sleep in the shade, wrapped up in big cloaks, if they are not lucky enough to get inside the hospital themselves. There was a handsome Arab who

A gate in Nazareth

haunted the place for a fortnight, waiting for his little son to recover from pneumonia, after having brought him from Trans-Jordan for treatment at the hospital. The matron told me that years ago, before there were any 'buses, a grannie carried a sick baby of some months old, in a wooden cradle, *on her head*, over twenty miles to the hospital.

One day the doctor took me down into the town in his car. At the foot of the long drive an Arab woman stopped the car. With tears running down her face, she told him that her little son was ill, and asked him to come and see him. The doctor agreed to this and the woman snatched his hand and kissed it, and put it to her forehead in the Arab greeting. Just so must people have waited for Christ, to ask Him to go and heal their children.

It was through a doctor at the hospital that I was enabled to go to Meshed, a village which I should certainly not otherwise have seen. He had been there to visit a patient, and had seen the interiors of the houses, which are peculiar to that district and particularly interesting. Three of us went in a car, with an Arab nurse in uniform.

Meshed is about eight miles from Nazareth, and is never visited by tourists, as it is quite off the track. Some of the villagers had been patients in the hospital, and they were familiar with, and respected, the nurse's uniform. She could tell them what we wanted to do.

The women took us round to see three or four of the houses, and we were followed, of course, by the whole village. As we passed through the low doorways, frightened hens flew out over our heads, clucking wildly.

The houses are built of mud and stone, and consist of one large room with an arched roof. In the thickness of the walls are recesses and shelves in which simple

View across the plain of Jezreel. 'We crossed the great plain of Jezreel, or Esdraelon – miles of flat country, surrounded by hills, with Mount Tabor's conical shape rising far on the northern side. This place is one of the great battle-grounds of the world, and abounds with names familiar in Bible history.'

Margaret W. Tarrant

An interior of a house at Meshed, near Cana of Galilee

necessities are stored. The walls are decorated with borders and panels of rough plaster designs in relief, some are geometrical and some are more suggestive of 'freehand' patterns. In many cases these decorations are done by the women, and the patterns, no doubt, are traditional. It was one of the most exciting and hardworking afternoons I have ever spent; there was so much to do, and so little time to do it. I drew three interiors, and one or two of the outside of houses, and sketched and took photographs of some of the people.

The last house we visited was the largest, and probably belonged to the head-man of the village. When I went in, I was amazed at the wonderful, almost theatrical effect. It was a large, high-pitched room, with its arched roof almost invisible in gloom and smoke. On the arches and on panels between them, there were plaster designs similar to those we had seen in other houses. The floor, a sort of platform of hardened mud, was raised about three feet from the ground, and was reached by three rough steps. Built into the front of the platform was a hollowed trough or manger, also of mud, and while we were working, a donkey came in at the door, pushed past us, and went to the manger for his evening meal. In the centre of the floor there was a fire in a big bowl, with a black pot over it, and beside it stood a woman, almost invisible in the darkness; every now and then she stooped and stirred the pot, the firelight flickering on her face and bent figure. On the floor, cross-legged, sat an old, old woman, very still and stiff, and by her a little child. One just wanted to sit and study that scene for hours.

Before we left, a girl of about sixteen came in; she had previously been a patient at the hospital in Nazareth, and recognized the nurse's uniform. She rushed up to us, and seized our hands, kissed them, and put them to her forehead, then squatted on the raised floor and

A woman near Nazareth

began sifting grain through a straw mat or sieve.

As in Jerusalem, the 'suk', or bazaar, of Nazareth is endlessly interesting, and full of pictures. One could, and does, spend hours looking at the tiny shops, and watching the people. I wanted to buy some native garments, and went into one shop where the man spoke a little English. He invited me to sit in a space behind the counter and gave me a cigarette to smoke while he attended to other customers. So I enjoyed a few minutes looking at various interesting garments such as belts

Goat-herds near Galilee

A carpenter's shop in Nazareth

and scarves stored on the shelves, and also in watching the keen faces of the Arab women intent on making purchases. I was soon the possessor of a beautiful brown camel-hair 'abbiyeh', and various other items which were made into a bundle and sent home on the back of the Hospital donkey.

If one climbs to the top of the flower-covered hills behind Nazareth, one is rewarded by a most glorious view of the surrounding country, in every direction. To the south, across the great plain, lie the misty 'hills that stand about Jerusalem'; to the west, the long line of Mount Carmel, and a blue strip of the Mediterranean; and to the north, line upon line of hills, topped by Mount Hermon, with its white streaks of snow; and to the east, the Jordan valley and the strange desolate-looking country of Trans-Jordan.

On the Nazarene hills, towards evening, you may see herds of agile black goats and kids, coming home for the night, accompanied by equally agile little goat-herds, who race about among the flowers and leap on the rocks, deftly throwing small stones at their charges to keep them from wandering. You may hear a strange, thin tune played on a pipe which one of the boys carries. Perhaps it is only a metal tube with holes pierced in it – no mouthpiece – nothing. Blow it in any way you will, you cannot make a sound, and the boys gather round you and laugh at your efforts. In the evening sunlight, a lad of about twelve, dressed in white, rides a donkey through the flowers. He carries a sickle, and is coming home from working in the fields, calling greetings to the goat-herds as he rides placidly by. He makes one think of another Lad, who probably rode across those same hills in the sunset glow.

In the main street of Nazareth is Mary's well, which used to be the only source of water in the village, and which must have been a public well or fountain in the days when Jesus was a boy. The scene near this well in the evenings is most fascinating to watch. The men come home from work, walking, or riding on donkeys (sometimes, alas, on bicycles); with them are camels, carrying enormous swaying loads of grass or hay, so that they look almost like walking haystacks. The goats return from pasture, and here and there kids rush out of doorways to meet them, and there is a great bleating and baa-ing, as they try to find their mothers. The women and girls go to the well for water, and return with large jars on their heads, perfectly balanced, walking with a swinging step and beautiful poise.

Mount Tabor is an easy drive from Nazareth, and the ascent is made by a steep zig-zag road, with some exceedingly sharp bends and a deep drop on one side. On the summit is a beautiful modern Franciscan Church and Monastery, built on the ruins of a far older one. We were greeted by a French monk, who came to meet us, wearing an apron over his brown habit, his hands covered with green paint. He asked us which

Woman with water jar at Nazareth

language we spoke, and having washed his hands, proceeded to show us over the building. Later, he left us to look at the view from a balcony on the very edge of the rock. We looked across the flat country to a little hillside village on the other side. It was Nain, where Christ raised the widow's son.

Bedouin women making butter by the Sea of Galilee

While we were on the balcony, Brother Henri came running, telling us to come and see the storks. From the other side of the building looking north, the sky seemed full of them; there must have been many hundreds, and Brother Henri obviously enjoyed watching our pleasure at this display. Somehow they gave the impression of being attached by invisible strings of varied length to some centre; their flight crossed and recrossed, and yet seemed leisurely and ordered. It was an amazing and extraordinarily uplifting sight. Later, we saw many of them standing in the long grass by the side of the road, their creamy breast-feathers fluttering in the wind.

The distance from Nazareth to Tabgha, on the northern shore of the Sea of Galilee is about twenty-eight miles, and the road lies over high rolling uplands, between fields of ripening corn, and with splendid views across the distant hills. The road begins to descend in wide sweeping curves, and then suddenly the car stops: 'Galilee!' cries the Arab driver, and points downwards. There, far below, is a small deep-blue triangle, the first glimpse, between the hills, of that little, world-famous sea.

At the German Hospice at Tabgha, one can almost imagine one is at the Italian Lakes; the garden goes down in terraces to the water, and is bright with flowers, and sweet with the scent of orange and lemon blossoms. Beside the lake is a narrow tree-shaded walk. Here, very early in the morning, visitors to the hospice walk, read and meditate. It is a lovely peaceful spot to rest, after visiting the busy towns and hot streets, and one can hardly realize that once it was a thriving populous district, and that the water was busy with fishing boats.

A couple of miles beyond Tabgha lies what is left of Capernaum, the town which Christ made His centre

The Sea of Galilee and The Horns of Hattin

after leaving Nazareth, and where He gave many discourses and worked many miracles. One may see the remains of the Synagogue, with a few splendid columns still standing, and many fallen and broken ones, some steps, and most interesting fragments of carved ornaments. From the ruins it has been possible to make plans and drawings of the original building, which may be seen in an adjoining room. Nearby is the Mountain of the Beatitudes, where Our Lord gave His Sermon on the Mount, and below is the spot on the Sea of Galilee where He preached from a boat:

'And it came to pass, that, as the people pressed upon Him to hear the word of God, he stood by the lake of Gennesaret, and saw two ships standing by the lake; but the fishermen were gone out of them, and were washing their nets. And He entered into one of the ships, which was Simon's, and prayed him that he would thrust out a little from the land. And he sat down, and taught the people out of the ship.'

Luke V. 1-3.

At one point on the shore there is a little bay from which the human voice can be heard from the sea, right up on the surrounding hills. One can picture the people gathered there, on the shore, to 'hear the word of God' and One speaking to them from the boat 'thrust out a little from the land', his voice reaching even to those clustered in the fields beyond.

At 7.15 on Palm Sunday morning, about ten people gathered under the eucalyptus trees by the lakeside. It was warm and sunny and very quiet – only the sound of the breeze among the leaves, ducks quacking and little waves lapping on the stones. A young clergyman from Jerusalem held a communion service there. For the altar, he used a large stone; there were no eucharistic vessels, just a plate, a glass, wine from the table at the hospice and bread newly-baked from the Bedouin tents nearby. Instead of the Gospel for Palm Sunday he read St. John XXI. 1-14: the story of how, after His Resurrection, Jesus stood on the shore, and spoke to His disciples who had toiled all night without catching any fish. He told them to let down their nets on the right side, 'and now they were not able to draw it for the multitude of fishes'. This was one of the never-to-be-forgotten episodes of the trip.

The Bedouin Arabs, who live near the Hospice, are employed on the estate. Their tents are picturesque, and are no doubt very similar to those used in Bible times; they are woven of dark brown goat hair, with flexible rush matting dividing each tent into two parts with the matting rolled back from the doorway.

The many children amuse themselves by making long necklaces of the little white pointed shells found on the shore; they waylay tourists, asking for baksheesh and hoping to sell their handiwork. They are happy, impish, attractive children, very ready to laugh and be

Bedouin tents, Sea of Galilee

The Sea of Galilee looking towards Tiberias. 'One can picture the people gathered there, on the shore, to "hear the word of God" and One speaking to them from the boat "thrust out a little from the land".'

friendly, in spite of the language difficulty. Near the tents also are many large dogs, which rush out and bark as one passes by, and it requires a certain amount of fortitude to walk along and appear unconcerned, with one or two large, aggressive-looking dogs following close at one's heels. The bigger lads are goat-herds, and in the evening the high, clear notes of their pipes may be heard as they lead their flocks back from the hills, or take them down to the edge of the water to drink.

I should like to have seen one of the sudden storms which sweep across the lake with little warning. During my stay, however, the water was smooth and sparkling, sometimes a glorious blue, sometimes pale silver and grey, crossed with lines of blue or green, where a breeze ruffled the surface, and as one looked to the furthest distance – due south – water and hills melted together into the bright sky. There was only an occasional fishing-boat to be seen, or a fisherman flinging his net into the water from the shore. One man went through his preliminary actions for my benefit, and then demanded payment for his trouble, and he would not actually fling the net until he had the money safe. When I had given him a coin he sent the net flying out, wide and true across the water in a lovely circle – but I had used my last film, and so could not take a photograph! I never saw the fisherman again.

To watch the approach of night from one of the hills behind Tabgha is an unforgettable experience. All is peaceful, glowing and rich in the sunset light, and the spaces around one seem so vast in the evening stillness. The hills of Trans-Jordan turn deep rose-colour, while the shadows in their folds and creases are blue, and below them, richer and stronger blue, lies the lake. The nearer fields, covered with dried grass or ripening crops, are at first golden, then, as the sun sinks, the shadows creep upwards and envelop them in twilight,

while the far hills change slowly from heather-colour to purple velvet, and the first stars shine out of the infinity of the sky. A spark of light glimmers from a Bedouin tent, a goat-bell tinkles, a distant dog barks, a late bird calls, but soon all is still, and night falls on Galilee.

Back by the long road to Jerusalem, through Tiberias, over the uplands to Nazareth, across the great plain, and then by the winding road that crosses the hills surrounding Jerusalem; seeing so many spots where one would like to stay and explore – Jenin, Nablus and small villages among the hills.

A beggar in Bethlehem

Bethlehem is about five miles beyond Jerusalem, and lies high on the hills so that one can see it from afar. Some distance out of the city there is a well by the roadside – the Well of the Magi, from which it is said that the Wise Men first saw the end of their travels – the guiding star was stationary above the little town.

In Bethlehem, there is a French Hospital, where guests can stay in lofty cell-like rooms, under the cloisters, which surround a lovely garden. In the spring it is bright with irises, lilac, roses and passion flowers, and the French sisters, in their blue dresses and large white-winged caps, flit between the flowers, and up the

Bethlehem

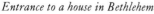
Entrance to a house in Bethlehem

wide steps to the beautiful church. The Arab nurses and servants speak French, and one almost forgets that one is not in France, until one sees the out-patients waiting to be admitted. Here indeed are the maimed, the halt, and the blind; Bedouin women in their strange black discoloured clothes and thick twisted turban-like headdresses, their hands and faces tattooed; poor shapeless bundles of rags squatting in the cool paved vestibule or in the dust, under the shadow of the high wall outside; women of Bethlehem with elaborately embroidered dresses and heavy rows of coins on their heads; all sorts and conditions gather here each morning to receive the kindly attentions of doctors and sisters.

High on the roof of the church stands a beautiful figure of the Redeemer, glowing against the blue sky, His hand stretched out over the little town where He was born.

In Bethlehem is the Church of the Nativity where people of various creeds may worship, but where they do not always agree. In a little chapel under the chancel, approached by a flight of semi-circular steps, is the Grotto of the Nativity. Here there is an altar, and, on the floor beneath it, a silver star let into the ground. This is the spot, it is said, where Jesus was born.

I had read so much about this Church, and expected it to be rather overdecorated, with many lamps and altars, but really it is lovely, and one could paint many pictures there. On my first visit, there was a service in progress; it was dusk, and the main part of the church was dark and gloomy and practically empty, but a raised chancel at the further end was crowded with people, and lighted by many lamps and candles. The women nearly all wore white head-veils, which looked almost blue in the dusk, while the lights illuminated their faces as they followed the service and chanted their responses. It was a wonderful effect of colour.

Women carrying earth from excavations in Bethlehem

There always seems to be a feeling of Christmas in the Church of the Nativity, with its huge candelabra shaped rather like Christmas trees, and long chains looped from one lamp to another, decorated with balls of varying sizes. Bethlehem seems a happy place, as it should be.

The Mount of Olives – Gethsemane – The Brook Cedron – The Garden Tomb – what pictures these

Margaret W. Tarrant

In the Temple Area, Jerusalem

Come and see the place where the Lord lay, painted as a result of the artist's trip to Palestine, displays a strong affinity with the artist's earlier painting of *The Garden Tomb* (see facing page) which, with her other sketches, provided an important source of reference for her later religious compositions.

names bring to one's imagination! Some prove to be more or less true pictures – others untrue. To one visitor a certain spot will seem full of reality and to be there will be one of the greatest moments of his life, while to another that place may be disappointing, but some others will satisfy him, and make his pilgrimage all that he hoped.

From the Mount of Olives one looks down on to Jerusalem, with its white buildings, flat roofs, minarets, the Dome of the Rock, and the great expanse of the Temple Area. In the evening light especially, it is a most beautiful view, and many thoughts come to mind. Jesus must have seen something very similar, as He looked down on to the city, and, foreseeing and foretelling its fate, wept over it. (Luke XIX. 37-44)

The Garden of Gethsemane is much nearer to the wall of the city than I had expected; there is only the very narrow valley of the Brook Cedron between. The Garden is divided and walled and fenced, and it is all so different from what one had imagined, but still there is quiet, and one may walk there among flowers and under trees. Who can tell how long those hoary olives have stood there? They live to a very great age, and one wonders what they witnessed in the Garden when they were young. When Our Lord went to the Garden of Gethsemane that night, and prayed, He must have looked across at the hill of Golgotha, outside the city wall, and have realised what was so soon to happen there:

'Oh my Father, if it be possible, let this cup pass from me! Nevertheless, not as I will, but as Thou wilt.'
Matthew XXVI. 39

Outside Jerusalem, there is another quiet garden, with a green door, and on the door is written 'I AM THE RESURRECTION AND THE LIFE'. On ringing the bell, a custodian admits visitors, and, if desired, leaves them to wander in the garden unattended. All is still and peaceful, and well cared-for. At the further end there is a rock-hewn tomb, thought by many to be the actual sepulchre of Our Lord.

In some such tomb as this His Body was laid; in some such quiet garden He conquered death, put behind Him the torture and agony and blackness of those last days, and rose again.

The Church of the Holy Sepulchre in Jerusalem is hallowed by the faith and love and prayers of countless thousands of pilgrims, but by the garden tomb, the scene of the Resurrection seems very real, and one may picture the Marys coming 'very early in the morning, when it was yet dark', and may think of One who walked in a garden in the first Easter dawn, while the birds sang to Him.

To travel from Jerusalem to Jericho by the 'old road' is a very romantic experience. The desert is the most extraordinary country one can imagine — even photographs give very little idea of it. The tremendous heat and glare, the brownish, sandy, rocky ground, the great hills and tortuous valleys, and the almost complete absence of vegetation, make the drive a continual marvel.

Now and then one sees herds of goats, black specks on the distant hill-side, led by a goat-herd, and all scintillating in the great heat. What do animals find there to eat? They must walk for miles in that sun-baked land in search of food, for the only plants are tiny grey dried-up bushes here and there among the stones.

By leaving the road at one point, and walking to the top of a hill, one can look down into a deep gorge. Built into the side of a mountain is the Convent of Conziba, or Deir el-Qelt. There has been a monastery here at least since the fourth century, and it is now occupied by Greek monks. A tiny road clinging to the side of the gorge leads to Jericho, and at the bottom of the valley there is a narrow stream, the only water, apparently, for miles around, all the other water-courses — wadis — seeming quite dry.

Jericho lies in the valley of the Jordan, and in olden times was famed for its palms and gardens. Now only a small portion of the district is cultivated, but where the soil is properly irrigated, it is still extremely fertile. On either side rise the hills of the desert, and a few miles to the south lies the Dead Sea, into which the Jordan flows. The sea is 1,292 feet below the level of the Mediterranean. It is 47 miles long and its greatest depth is 1,310 feet. The water contains a high percentage of various salts, and there is now a chemical factory at the northern end. The stones on the edge of the water, and the landing places, glitter with the dried salt, and give the appearance of sparkling frost, but the atmosphere suggests anything but winter.

Sunset light on the Hills of Moab. The harshness and heat of Palestine is superbly captured in this panorama of the Dead Sea, and illustrates the artist's appreciation of the senses of strangeness and beauty that complement each other throughout her diary.

It is indeed a dead sea, strange and deserted, the bare hills of Moab – range upon range, rising out of the water on the Eastern side, with their deep creases and gorges – no boats, or fish, or birds, or trees, simply stillness, colour, pulsing heat, and – uncanniness.

Back to Jerusalem by the 'new road'. The desert is left behind, but how much more real – and terrible – will the account of those 'forty days and forty nights' always seem, now that one has seen the country where 'Jesus was led up of the spirit into the wilderness'.

Times have been difficult, lately, for Palestine; troubles and riots and bloodshed. One cannot wonder that such things should be, having seen the people, and realising what a terrible task it must be to control and govern them, and to satisfy both Arab and Jew. The Holy City – what a marvellous story it could tell!

Nazareth

Jerusalem

Historical Note

Margaret Tarrant's perceptive last paragraph, her only reference to the turbulent politics of the Holy Land, is just as relevant today, more than 50 years after her visit. In 1917 the British Government had officially proposed the establishment in Palestine of a national home for the Jewish people (The Balfour Declaration) and in 1920 the League of Nations put Palestine under a British Mandate, which lasted until the State of Israel was founded in 1948. During the 1930s the British were not popular either with the Jews or with the Arabs. In 1929 serious anti-British riots were repressed and in 1936 a proposal by the British for a partition of Jewish and Arab areas was rejected by the Arabs.